CLOSER TO

MY

DREAMS

TORINER HALE

Dedication

I would like to dedicate this book to myself first and foremost. To the quiet yet tenacious little girl from East Baltimore, Maryland who overcame much adversity.Now an aspiring first time Author, Poet, and mother of two loving, beautiful, and multi-talented children. Of whom I love, admire, and cherish with all of my heart. Along with our little feisty favorite girl in the whole wide world our family dog.You all have been my greatest inspirations. You all mean the world to me.

This book is also dedicated to my one and only sharp-witted wonderful sister, who has always believed in me. She has always been one of my loudest and greatest supporters. To my two amazingly talented nephews, I am so proud of the magnificent young men that you all are becoming. I love all of you more than you will ever know.

Author's Words of Inspiration: "Obstacles will always surely arise to slow down your process.However, always remember this is all apart of the process. Just relax and regroup.Don't give up! It's all apart of the test.Keep moving forward and you will progress."

Closer To My Dreams

A vision so far, but yet so near

Just a thought last night

But now you are here

Closer to my dreams

A year filled with depression and fear

Anxiety built up inside for the loss of things that I've
held oh so dear

Has made everything all so clear

Closer to my dreams

The fact of the matter

Is that dreams sometimes do splatter

However it's up to you to continue to climb that ladder

If you don't your dreams soon won't matter

So hold on and don't let your dreams shatter

For I am Closer to My Dreams

What A Place

Your mind and the thoughts it holds.

Memories sometimes can be worth more than gold

Like cruising through a tunnel then stopping to
pay the toll.

If you sit still long enough you can watch them unfold

Just imagine living your life this bold

Look at you now you're on a roll

Sense of Care

Is very rare

It's something that we all don't share

And to experience this love is so debonair

For you'll always feel that sense of care

Simply knowing that it's always near

A Fathers Love

Never wavers or folds

A father's love provides warmth when we are cold

He loves us more even when we turn old

His kisses are worth more than gold

In his hands our tiny hearts he will forever hold

Rare

Often you do things for others without a care

Even when you only have little time to spare

Always committing selfless acts that others
wouldn't dare

Reaching higher levels because you know the
significance of what it means to share

Above all people can always depend on you to be there

Just a few reasons why you're rare

A Strong Man

Holds his head up high because he can

A strong man, has the strength of many men

He doesn't turn his head, he embraces the wind

Facing pain and adversity, as only a strong man can

Meeting You

Meeting you has been nothing ordinary

For you my heart has an unexplainable love
that it carries

Being in your presence is like my own sanctuary

Because you are so extraordinary

Amazing

The little things you do and say

Makes me want to stay

The soothing sound of your voice

Makes me glad I'm your choice

Your different style of swag

Makes me want to brag

About this amazing man

That has fell in my hands

Where I Wanna Be

In your arms with your sensuous charm

Feeling as if you can do no harm

Blocking out all of life's numerous wrongs

Moved by the thought that this has lasted this long

Thinking of another meaningful song

That reminds me of our special bond

I Dreamed a Little Dream of You

While these feelings are semi old

At times they seem so new

Me thinking about you

As I often do

My mind wandering in and outta space

Envisions of your attractive face

Often my heart begins to race

Just thinking about your smile and grace

A True Love

A true love is wonderful and bold

It never wavers or folds

A true love provides lots of tender love and care

For it is pure and very rear

A true love is just like a bird on a wire

Breathing life into you, as it lifts you higher and higher

A true love will never bring you stress

It takes great pride in you enjoying your rest, while
basking in your soothing caress

A true love will put you to the test

All because it's meant to bring out your best

A true love holds so much desire

Because it can truly set your soul afire

A true love is supposed to grow

To take you places only you and your true love should
know

In My Mind

Time moves at a speeding pace

Often off on its own race

Then sometimes gone without a trace

Unfortunately, it doesn't know that I don't like to chase

I'd rather sit still and be comfortable in my own space

Why must my thoughts be all over the place

Is it because it likes my poker face

Or my smile that offers much style and grace

A Special Place

Is laying in your arms and being caressed

Comfortably resting my head on
your chest

Inhaling your calming scent as you peacefully rest

With me gently rubbing on your arms
and bare chest

While thinking about what
I could have done to become so blessed

Time

Stands still for no one

Not even when you think you've won

There's always that last thing that you always could have
done

Seemly knowing that something else will surely come

Beating along to the sound of a huge drum

Just as sure as the earth orbits around the sun

Time stands still for no one

Memories

Come and go

Fast and slow

Oh how they go

Memories

They're here

And there

They're everywhere

Oh those memories

Why art thou memories?

No one seems to know

Why memories grow fast

And seem to die so slow

Memories

The Rain

Sometimes eases the pain

When there are no words that can be explained

Oh how we try to avoid the rain

That makes us face those strains

But the rain sometimes brings a comfort so that
we can sustain

All of the formalities of lives inevitable pains.

Life

Some how has many twists and turns

And if you are not careful you may suffer many burns

Then you'll find yourself wondering what have you
learned

Weaving in and out of consciousness as your mind tries
so hard to unlearn

As your life flips upside down your body starts to
squirm

Thinking about all of the things in life that you've
yearned

Really were of little to no concern

2020

The year of the crazies

A time the world opened up as Fugazi

Our lives went from running raggedy to just being lazy

Foreshadowed by a lot of maybes

Oh, how our lives look so wavy

Completely turned upside down

Then unexpected people being shady

Oh but, 2020 you won't break me

The Sun

Shines so bright

Whenever you feel as though you've lost your way just
look to this light

Keep walking with your head held high and pushing
with all your might

Don't throw in the towel, keep fighting the fight

Just sit back, relax and watch those gray sky's turn into
beautiful night's

Made in the USA
Middletown, DE
11 February 2021

32612762R00015